LIVE OR DIE?

SURVIVAL HACKS

BONNIE BURTON

Brimming with creative inspiration, how-to projects, and useful
information to enrich your everyday life, Quarto Knows is a favorite
destination for those pursuing their interests and passions. Visit our
site and dig deeper with our books into your area of interest:
Quarto Creates, Quarto Cooks, Quarto Homes, Quarto Lives,
Quarto Drives, Quarto Explores, Quarto Gifts, or Quarto Kids.

18 19 20 21 22   5 4 3 2 1

ISBN: 978-0-7603-6470-3

Library of Congress Cataloging-in-Publication Data available upon request.

Author: Bonnie Burton
Design: Scott Richardson
Editorial: Jill Saginario
Production: Shawn Reed

Printed, manufactured, and assembled in Shenzhen, China, 10/18.

Distributed by:
Scholastic Inc., New York, NY 10012
Scholastic Canada Ltd., Markham, Ontario L6C 1Z7

Image credits:
Page 6: Sailboat aproaching to the glacier San Rafael ©Fotografías Jorge León Cabello/ Getty Images; Page 18: Inuit
Man Wearing Snow Goggles ©Marilyn Angel Wynn/ Getty Images; Page 22: Plane Crash Survivors at Lean-To Camp
©Bettmann/ Getty Images; Page 40: Airplane crash survivor Juliane Kopcke ©Bettmann/ Getty Images; Page 58: Water
sign and cow skull in the desert ©Robin Smith/ Getty Images; Page 68: A woman with mirror in the woods ©Kei Uesugi/
Getty Images; Page 71: Woman wearing support stockings ©Phanie/ Alamy Stock Photo; Page 76: A Boy Scout sets
up a camping tent ©Robb Reece/ Getty Images; Page 77: Volunteers Scott Byrd, John Beamer and Lisa Byrd strike out
©Charlotte Observer/ Getty Images; Page 79: Island Storm ©Joel Sharpe/ Getty Images.
All other photographs and design elements ©Shutterstock.com

306222

TABLE OF CONTENTS

HOW TO USE THIS BOOK 4

ARCTIC. 7

JUNGLE 24

DESERT 42

FOREST. 60

TROPICAL ISLAND 78

HOW TO MAKE YOUR OWN COMPASS 95

INDEX 96

HOW TO USE THIS BOOK

THIS BOOK PROVIDES EASY-TO-FOLLOW STEPS TO TURN ORDINARY ITEMS YOU ALREADY OWN IN YOUR BACKPACK INTO SURVIVAL TOOLS. PACKED WITH USEFUL FACTS, REAL-LIFE SURVIVAL EXAMPLES, AND CREATIVE HACKS, THIS HANDBOOK IS INDISPENSABLE IF YOU FIND YOURSELF STRANDED ALL ALONE IN AN EXTREME TERRAIN.

THE TERRAIN

Each terrain requires different priorities for survival. Whether your plane crash-landed in the jungle, or you get separated from your hiking buddies in the forest, the hacks in this book will help you decide which task to tackle first to help you survive until help arrives.

Warning: This book has great advice, but never put yourself in dangerous situations just to test out whether our tips work in the real world. The publisher cannot accept responsibility for any injuries, damages, loss, or lawsuits resulting from the information in this book.

THE CHALLENGES

Each challenge comes with handy illustrations, facts, and tips that will make beating survival challenges a breeze. Plus read dramatic real-life survival stories for inspiration.

THE HACKS

Even if you have a tent, matches, or any other real survival gear . . . you still have your backpack full of things you may not have realized are actually useful.

CAN YOU SURVIVE DANGEROUS TERRAINS?

Getting lost can be frightening, especially when it's in a landscape you're not familiar with. This book will help you survive in unusual places such as the arctic, the jungle, the desert, the forest, and a tropical island.

While this book will show you how to transform everyday objects into useful gear, remember that your number one survival tool is your brain. Always use common sense . . . and you may just make it out alive!

ARCTIC ISOLATION

OH NO!

Your parents drag you on a sailing trip to see the polar bears. But your ship pulled a Titanic and now you have found yourself in the hazardous situation of being stranded on a sheet of ice. There's also seems to be a blizzard brewing on the horizon. As the snow piles on, your body temperature drops. If you wish to make it through the night, you will have to beat the cold. But how?

YOUR CHALLENGES

IN YOUR BACKPACK, YOU HAVE AN UNUSUAL ASSORTMENT OF ODDS AND ENDS LIKE A BOOK, SPARE CHANGE, AND EYEGLASSES. NONE OF THESE ITEMS WILL HELP YOU GATHER FOOD, STAY WARM, OR PROTECT YOU FROM THE HARSH ENVIRONMENT. OR WILL THEY?

Challenge 1 — **KEEP WARM**

Challenge 2 — **FIND FOOD**

Challenge 3 — **STAY HYDRATED**

Challenge 4 — **BUILD A SHELTER**

Challenge 5 — **COMBAT SNOW BLINDNESS**

Challenge 6 — **CONQUER SNOW TRAVEL**

Hacks from Your Pack

IN THE PACK:

1. NICKEL
2. BOOK
3. RULER
4. TENNIS RACKETS
5. SODA CAN
6. EYEGLASSES
7. SANDWICH BAG

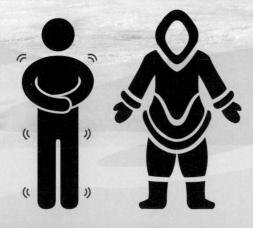

CHALLENGE 1:
KEEP WARM

YOUR NUMBER ONE PRIORITY FOR SURVIVAL IS TO BEAT THE ARCTIC TEMPERATURES AND PREVENT GETTING AN ABNORMALLY LOW BODY TEMPERATURE THAT COULD LEAD TO HYPOTHERMIA AND FROSTBITE.

THE BEST WAY TO FEND OFF THE COLD IS TO BUILD A FIRE. GATHER ANY DRY WOOD, STICKS, OR BRANCHES. USE PAPER OR MOSS AS FAST-BURNING TINDER TO PLACE AROUND THE WOOD. REMEMBER TO ALWAYS HAVE PLENTY OF DRY KINDLING READY TO KEEP YOUR FIRE GOING THROUGHOUT THE DAY AND NIGHT.

| Branches | Sticks | Paper | Moss |

IN THE PACK:

1. NICKEL
2. BOOK
3. RULER
4. TENNIS RACKETS
5. SODA CAN
6. **EYEGLASSES**
7. SANDWICH BAG

Hacks from Your Pack

EYEGLASSES

If you wear magnifying eyeglasses, you can focus the sun's rays to ignite tinder.

STEP 1

Gather tinder and place around firewood.

STEP 2

Use the lens to concentrate the sun's rays on the tinder to ignite it.

STEP 3

Gently blow on the tinder when it starts smoking.

BONUS HACK

You can also use ice as a makeshift magnifying glass to start a fire. The ice must be totally clear and shaped into a sphere.

CHALLENGE 2: FIND FOOD

IN WARMER CONDITIONS YOU CAN SURVIVE UP TO SIXTY DAYS WITHOUT FOOD. BUT IN EXTREME COLD TEMPERATURES, YOU MIGHT ONLY LAST A COUPLE OF WEEKS IF USING A LOT OF ENERGY. SO IT PAYS TO WORK SMARTER, NOT HARDER. THE FASTER YOU BURN CALORIES, THE MORE CRUCIAL IT IS TO FIND THINGS TO EAT, QUICKLY. DON'T FORGET TO DRINK AS MUCH WATER AS POSSIBLE TO PREVENT DEHYDRATION.

IN THE PACK:

1. NICKEL
2. BOOK
3. RULER
4. TENNIS RACKETS
5. SODA CAN
6. EYEGLASSES
7. SANDWICH BAG

Hacks from Your Pack

NICKEL

A nickel may not be worth much, but it can be indispensable for catching fish once you've fashioned it into a spear! Almost all Arctic sea life comes to the surface of the water eventually, so punch through a hole in the ice and wait for your dinner to come to you.

STEP 1

Use a rock to pound the nickel until it's thinner and flatter on one side.

STEP 2

Scrape the rock alongside the flattened side, so you can file it into a sharp point.

STEP 3

Pound only the middle until there is a bit of a neck shape.

STEP 4

Once you have transformed the coin into an arrowhead, use strips of bark or your shoelace to fasten it to the end of a stick.

SPEAR FISHING TIPS

THE KEY TO SUCCESSFUL SPEAR FISHING IS BEING ABLE TO SEE WHAT IS GOING ON IN THE WATER—HOW ELSE ARE YOU GOING TO SEE THE FISH? TRY TO FIND A SPOT WITH CLEAR WATER AND A DARK, SANDY BOTTOM. STAY QUIET AND MOTIONLESS SO YOU DON'T SCARE AWAY CURIOUS FISH. ONCE YOU SPOT ONE, THROW THE SPEAR AT THE FISH WHEN IT IS FACING AWAY FROM YOU. THIS WILL REDUCE THE ODDS OF THE FISH SEEING YOU MOVE WHEN THROWING THE SPEAR.

GATHERING FOOD WITHOUT A HEARTBEAT

If fishing makes you too queasy, there are more than 1,700 species of plant life thriving in the Arctic tundra—many of them edible, including lingonberries, bilberries, blueberries, alpine bearberries, and apples.

TIP: Never eat a plant you can't identify!

Lingonberries

Bilberries

Blueberries

Alpine Bearberries

Apples

CHALLENGE 3: STAY HYDRATED

WATER IS EVERYWHERE IN THE ARCTIC, EVEN IF IT'S IN THE FORM OF ICE AND SNOW. THE ICE OF THE ARCTIC CONTAINS AROUND TEN PERCENT OF THE WORLD'S FRESH WATER.

EVERY PART OF YOUR BODY, FROM CELLS TO ORGANS, DEPENDS ON WATER TO SURVIVE. WATER EVEN HELPS YOUR BODY REGULATE TEMPERATURE.

FROZEN FACTS!

Typical survival gear doesn't always work in extremely cold temperatures. Portable cooking devices are useless because butane fuel will never warm up enough to change from a liquid to a gas. Plastic becomes brittle and may shatter.

IN THE PACK:

1. NICKEL
2. BOOK
3. RULER
4. TENNIS RACKETS
5. **SODA CAN**
6. EYEGLASSES
7. SANDWICH BAG

Hacks from Your Pack

SODA CAN

Collect ice or snow using the empty can. You'll then need to melt the contents of the can before consuming or you'll lose body heat. Boiling the water in the soda can over a flame has the added benefit of purifying the water.

Hacks from Your Pack

EYEGLASSES & SANDWICH BAG

In cases where you can't make a fire, you can speed up the melting process using the lens from your eyeglasses to focus the sun's rays. But caution—this only works if you wear reading glasses! If you don't have a fire handy, pack snow and ice inside a bag stashed between layers of your clothing—your own body heat will slowly melt the ice and snow into water that you can drink later.

IN THE PACK:

1. NICKEL
2. BOOK
3. RULER
4. TENNIS RACKETS
5. SODA CAN
6. **EYEGLASSES**
7. **SANDWICH BAG**

CHALLENGE 4: BUILD A SHELTER

A TRENCH DUG IN THE SNOW CREATES AN INSULATED AREA HANDY FOR SLEEPING OR JUST FOR WAITING UNTIL YOU ARE RESCUED. DIG A SIMPLE PIT NEAR THE BASE OF A TREE, THEN LINE THE PIT WITH PINE BOUGHS OR GRASS FOR ADDED INSULATION. SNOW ITSELF CAN ALSO TURN OUT TO BE ONE OF YOUR BEST PROTECTIONS AGAINST THE WIND.

BONUS HACK

Covering a trench or a pit with bright clothing like a shirt is also smart so people can spot you better from the air when looking for you in the white, snow-covered landscape.

IN THE PACK:

1. NICKEL
2. BOOK
3. **RULER**
4. TENNIS RACKETS
5. SODA CAN
6. EYEGLASSES
7. SANDWICH BAG

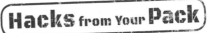
RULER

This long piece of wood can serve as a crude tool for shoveling snow, as well as for measuring the thickness of your snow cave to make sure it's sturdy enough to withstand cold winds.

STEP 1

Dig a hole into the snow.

STEP 2

Build a snow cave with walls about eight inches thick.

STEP 3

Use a stick to create angled ventilation holes in the roof.

STEP 4

Create a packed snow door to cover the entrance.

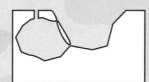

STEP 5

Make sure there are ventilation holes in the door as well.

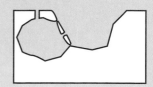

STEP 6

Inside your homemade cave, scrape the snow down to ground level to take advantage of radiant heat from the soil.

CHALLENGE 5:
COMBAT SNOW BLINDNESSS

SNOW BLINDNESS CAUSES A LOSS OF VISION WHEN YOUR CORNEA BECOMES SUNBURNED DUE TO OVEREXPOSURE TO THE SUN'S INVISIBLE, BUT POWERFUL, UV RAYS REFLECTING OFF THE SNOW AND ICE.

SYMPTOMS OF SNOW BLINDNESS INCLUDE BURNING EYES, RED EYES, A FEELING THAT SOME KIND OF GRIT OR SAND IS IN YOUR EYE, SENSITIVITY TO LIGHT, WATERY EYES, BLURRY VISION, SWOLLEN EYES AND EYELIDS, SEVERE HEADACHE, AND SEEING HALOS AROUND LIGHTS.

IF YOU CAN'T SEE AT ALL, DON'T PANIC! VISION LOSS DUE TO SNOW BLINDNESS IS ONLY TEMPORARY AND TYPICALLY RESOLVES ITSELF IN 24 TO 48 HOURS.

Inuit snow goggle made from bone.

IN THE PACK:

1. NICKEL
2. **BOOK**
3. RULER
4. TENNIS RACKETS
5. SODA CAN
6. EYEGLASSES
7. SANDWICH BAG

Hacks from Your Pack

BOOK

The easiest way to prevent snow blindness is to wear sunglasses during the daylight hours. Avoid suffering from the sun's glare bouncing off the snow using these makeshift sunglasses.

STEP 1
Tear off the cover of a book.

STEP 2
Cut 1/8" slit vertically.

STEP 3
Punch a small hole at both ends.

STEP 4
Tie the cover to your face using your shoelaces or strips of thin bark.

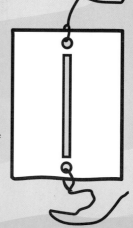

CHALLENGE 6:
CONQUER SNOW TRAVEL

THE SNOW WILL BE THE BIGGEST OBSTACLE WHILE TRAVELING ON FOOT, ESPECIALLY IF YOU PLAN ON WALKING A LONG DISTANCE—LIKE FOLLOWING A NEARBY STREAM IN ORDER TO FIND SIGNS OF CIVILIZATION.

FASHION SNOWSHOES OUT OF WHATEVER IS AT YOUR DISPOSAL. YOU'LL WANT TO USE SOMETHING THAT WILL KEEP YOU ON THE TOP OF THE SNOW, INSTEAD OF SINKING INTO IT.

BE SAFE ON ICE

You'll want to walk on snow instead of ice, but if you plan on fishing or collecting ice to melt for water, you have to be extra careful where you step. That frozen lake, river, or stream may look solid enough to walk across, but if you plunge through the ice, it can have dire results—especially if you are all alone.

✗ Don't even think of stepping on any ice unless the outside temperature is 20°F or lower.

✗ Do not step on black ice. It is newly formed thin ice and you will probably fall through.

Check your path first with a sturdy stick to tap the surface and test how solid it is. If the ice sounds hollow when tapped, choose another path. Repeated use weakens ice, so if you're following someone else's tracks on the ice, watch out for cracks.

 Gray ice is considered to be "young ice" and is usually between 4 to 6 inches thick. It should support your weight but it's best to avoid standing on if possible.

 White ice, which is roughly 6 to 12 inches thick, is the safest to walk on.

STEP 1

Place your boot in the center of each tennis racket.

STEP 2

Untie the laces from your boot and re-tie, lashing the shoe to the racket frame.

STEP 3

For extra stability, tear a piece of cloth into strips and tie the heel of the boot to the racket at its widest point.

IN THE PACK:

1. NICKEL
2. BOOK
3. RULER
4. **TENNIS RACKETS**
5. SODA CAN
6. EYEGLASSES
7. SANDWICH BAG

Hacks from Your Pack

TENNIS RACKETS

One of the fastest ways to make snowshoes is to use rackets. If rackets aren't readily available, you can also craft homemade snowshoes using branches you find on the ground.

NEVER WANDER OFF ALONE!

If you plan to leave your camp, bring at least one other person with you. This serves as an extra smart precaution in case one of you ends up suffering from snow blindness or falls through the ice.

If you are alone, at least leave a note at your temporary shelter explaining where you've gone and describing the direction, so that rescuers have a better chance of locating you.

Gone Fishing!

REAL-LIFE SURVIVAL STORY
The Downed Plane

In the winter of 1963, a small plane crashed in the Canadian Yukon, stranding a female passenger with a broken arm and the pilot, who had a broken jaw. They had no heavy winter clothes, and their supplies consisted of a few cans of sardines and tuna, two cans of fruit cocktail, vitamins, toothpaste, and matches.

With only a few tools—a hammer, a chisel, and the pilot's hunting knife—they managed to use the plane's cabin with added spruce boughs as a shelter. They made a drinking cup from a broken light reflector to drink melted snow and avoided any major physical activity so their bodies' stored fat could sustain them after the food ran out. When found by rescuers forty-nine days later, they were thin and hungry, but alive.

Visiting the campsite made by the survivors of the Yukon plane crash.

REAL-LIFE SURVIVAL STORY
The Trapped Car

In 2012, a middle-aged man who was trapped for two months near the Arctic Circle was found alive, thanks to his car. The temperature outside was -22°F (-30°C) but because his car became a kind of accidental igloo it kept the temperature inside a more tolerable 0°F (-17°C).

A car igloo may save your life!

TERRAIN 02: JUNGLE

JUNGLE FACTS!

Jungles and rainforests are similar. However, rainforests have thick canopies of tall trees that block out light, while jungles allow more light in, making it easier for plants to grow and animals to flourish.

Animals that dwell in jungles include howler monkeys, tigers, jaguars, and dangerous snakes like cobras. Elephants, rhinoceroses, and water buffalo can also be found in certain jungles.

A four-square-mile (ten-square-km) area of a jungle can contain as many as 1,500 species of flowering plants, 750 species of trees, 400 species of birds, and 150 species of butterflies. Many types of plants in the jungle protect themselves from being eaten by giving off poisonous toxins if an animal should come too close.

Jungles are found all over the world. The most famous jungles are located in Central America and South America. Because they thrive in warm environments with hot and humid temperatures, jungles are typically found near the equator.

IT'S A JUNGLE OUT THERE

OH NO!

On your way to Costa Rica, your plane crosses paths with a flock of birds who get stuck in the engine and cause your plane to crash in the jungle. As the sole survivor, it's up to you to find a way back to civilization.

TERRAIN 02: JUNGLE

YOUR CHALLENGES

IF YOU HAVE A LARGE PLASTIC BAG, TIN CANS, AN ID CARD, A SALT PACKET, AND A ROLL OF DUCT TAPE, YOU'LL BE ABLE TO SURVIVE WHILE LOST IN THE JUNGLE.

BUT WHICH ITEMS WILL YOU CHOOSE TO HELP YOU STAY HEALTHY AND PRODUCTIVE UNTIL YOU CAN REACH CIVILIZATION AGAIN?

Challenge 1 COLLECT AND FILTER DRINKING WATER

Challenge 2 BUILD A TEMPORARY HOME

Challenge 3 FIGURE OUT YOUR LOCATION

Challenge 4 GRAB SOME DINNER

Challenge 5 FIRST AID

Challenge 6 LIGHT A FIRE

Hacks from Your Pack

IN THE PACK:

1. WRISTWATCH
2. TRASH BAG
3. SUPER GLUE
4. CAYENNE PEPPER
5. SALT PACKET
6. ID CARD
7. TIN CAN
8. SOCKS
9. DUCT TAPE
10. NEWSPAPER

CHALLENGE 1:
COLLECT AND FILTER DRINKING WATER

FINDING WATER IN THE JUNGLE IS A FAIRLY EASY TASK—JUST OBSERVE THE INSECTS. LARGE SWARMS OF INSECTS OFTEN INDICATE A NEARBY WATER SOURCE. BEES PREFER TO BUILD THEIR HIVES WITHIN A COUPLE OF MILES OF A BODY OF WATER, AND FLIES TYPICALLY STAY WITHIN 300 FEET OF WATER.

IN THE PACK:

1. WRISTWATCH
2. TRASH BAG
3. SUPER GLUE
4. CAYENNE PEPPER
5. SALT PACKET
6. ID CARD
7. TIN CAN
8. SOCKS
9. DUCT TAPE
10. NEWSPAPER

BONUS HACK!
Secret Water Stores

Bamboo plants also collect water during rainfall. Bend or poke holes in the bamboo rods to allow the water to flow out into the can.

Hacks from Your Pack

TIN CAN

The leaves of plants and trees in the jungle are so large that they can be used to collect rain water. Just funnel the water from a large leaf into a can from your sack and you will have sufficient water for later use.

Boil any water that you collect in order to kill any bacteria.

IN THE PACK:

1. WRISTWATCH
2. TRASH BAG
3. SUPER GLUE
4. CAYENNE PEPPER
5. SALT PACKET
6. ID CARD
7. TIN CAN
8. SOCKS
9. DUCT TAPE
10. NEWSPAPER

Hacks from Your Pack

SOCKS

You can use your socks to soak up dew or water from hard-to-reach places such as tree trunks or rock cracks. You can even make a water filter from a sock by pouring water through it to remove rock sediment.

CHALLENGE 2: BUILD A TEMPORARY HOME

TO SURVIVE IN THE JUNGLE, YOU HAVE TO BE ABLE TO PROTECT YOURSELF FROM WILDLIFE. YOU'RE VULNERABLE TO ANTS, SPIDERS, SCORPIONS, AND SNAKES—ESPECIALLY AT NIGHT. SO BUILDING A SHELTER IS CRUCIAL.

IN THE PACK:

1. WRISTWATCH
2. TRASH BAG
3. SUPER GLUE
4. CAYENNE PEPPER
5. SALT PACKET
6. ID CARD
7. TIN CAN
8. SOCKS
9. DUCT TAPE
10. NEWSPAPER

Hacks from Your Pack

TRASH BAG & DUCT TAPE

Ideally, you'd find an existing place that could serve as shelter rather than try to build one. If you can't find shelter in your area, seek out tall buttress roots of trees. You can then drape a big plastic trash bag over the "walls" of the roots to make a cozy shelter.

Buttress roots

STEP 1

Find a large tree with high buttress roots.

STEP 2

Twist a length of duct tape to form a rope and run between two walls of roots.

STEP 3

Drape the plastic bag over the rope.

STEP 4

Stake the sides of the plastic bag into the ground using sticks or heavy rocks.

CHALLENGE 3: FIGURE OUT YOUR LOCATION

YOU DON'T ALWAYS NEED A COMPASS TO FIGURE OUT WHERE YOU ARE IN A JUNGLE.

DON'T GET MORE LOST

To keep from walking in circles in the jungle, always walk in one general direction. Focus on a reference point in the distance to aim for.

Head downhill to look for a stream. Keep following it until it becomes a river, which will eventually lead you out of the jungle.

While walking, avoid grabbing vines or plants while making your way up a hill or incline. Many jungle plants have thorns that could injure you.

Leave piles of rocks along your trail so those who are looking for you will know which path you've taken.

IN THE PACK:

1. WRISTWATCH
2. TRASH BAG
3. SUPER GLUE
4. CAYENNE PEPPER
5. SALT PACKET
6. ID CARD
7. TIN CAN
8. SOCKS
9. DUCT TAPE
10. NEWSPAPER

Hacks from Your Pack

WRISTWATCH

This book includes the tools to make a homemade compass, but an analog watch will also do in a pinch! If you're in the southern hemisphere, north and south will be reversed.

STEP 1 Hold your watch with the dial facing up, while also parallel to the ground.

STEP 2 While keeping it level, turn the watch until the hour hand is pointing in the direction of the sun.

STEP 3 If it's morning, south should be about halfway between the hour hand and 12 o'clock, clockwise.

STEP 4 If it's afternoon, south lies about halfway between the hour hand and 12 o'clock, counterclockwise.

STEP 5 North will be on the same line but in the opposite direction.

Morning

Afternoon

BONUS HACK!

DIY Alarm System

Tie a few tin cans and lids to some dental floss or vines and string it across the perimeter of your camp or around your shelter. Floss is difficult to see, so animal intruders moving around near your camp will trip the floss, shaking the cans, which will alert you you're not alone.

CHALLENGE 4: GRAB SOME DINNER

FISHING IS AN EASY WAY TO EARN YOUR DINNER IN THE JUNGLE.

WHAT IS THERE TO EAT?

There are plenty of edible plants in the jungle.

Stick with palms, bamboo, and common fruits. Look for coconuts, squash, cucumber, cashews, peanuts, and citrus fruits, all of which are plentiful in many jungles.

TIP Watch monkeys to see what kinds of fruits and plants they eat. They will be safe for you to consume as well.

Worms, grubs, and termites are everywhere in the jungle and are all great protein sources.

TIP If you're able to find fruit, don't try to store it. Your pile of food will likely spoil quickly in the heat and humidity, and could attract animals and insects.

Before eating any produce, test the juice on your skin to see how it reacts. Usually bright red, white, or yellow berries and plants with a milky sap should be avoided.

Don't eat mushrooms. Some are safe, but many are highly toxic and even deadly, so it's not worth the risk if you don't already know which ones are poisonous.

Steer clear of brightly colored insects or bugs that are hairy or have stingers.

STEP 1
Find a long bamboo stalk to use as your spear.

STEP 2
Use a sharp rock to cut an X into the tip so that the end of the spear separates into 4 individual prongs.

STEP 3
Separate the prongs with vine to keep them apart.

STEP 4
Wrap the handle end in duct tape from your pack so you have a better grip on the spear.

STEP 5
Stand on a rock overlooking the river or stream. Remain still and quiet so you don't scare away the fish.

STEP 6
Wait for a fish to swim near you, then stab it with the spear to catch it.

IN THE PACK:

1 WRISTWATCH
2 TRASH BAG
3 SUPER GLUE
4 CAYENNE PEPPER
5 SALT PACKET
6 ID CARD
7 TIN CAN
8 SOCKS
9 DUCT TAPE
10 NEWSPAPER

Hacks from Your Pack

DUCT TAPE
This all-purpose item gives you the grip needed to become a spear fishing master.

CHALLENGE 5:
FIRST AID

THE JUNGLE IS FULL OF PRICKLY PLANTS AND OVERZEALOUS INSECTS. AT SOME POINT YOU WILL HAVE TO DO A BIT OF FIRST AID. IN YOUR PACK, THERE ARE PLENTY OF ITEMS TO FIX WOUNDS, HEAL INSECT BITES, AND REMOVE STINGERS.

IN THE PACK:

1. WRISTWATCH
2. TRASH BAG
3. SUPER GLUE
4. CAYENNE PEPPER
5. SALT PACKET
6. ID CARD
7. TIN CAN
8. SOCKS
9. DUCT TAPE
10. NEWSPAPER

Hacks from Your Pack

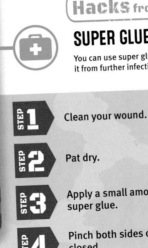

SUPER GLUE

You can use super glue to seal your wound and protect it from further infection.

STEP 1 Clean your wound.

STEP 2 Pat dry.

STEP 3 Apply a small amount of super glue.

STEP 4 Pinch both sides of the skin closed.

Hacks from Your Pack

CAYENNE PEPPER

This seasoning is great for spicing up bland food, but it also stops a cut from bleeding. Just pour a pile on the wound and the bleeding will stop in under ten seconds.

IN THE PACK:

1. WRISTWATCH
2. TRASH BAG
3. SUPER GLUE
4. CAYENNE PEPPER
5. SALT PACKET
6. ID CARD
7. TIN CAN
8. SOCKS
9. DUCT TAPE
10. NEWSPAPER

IN THE PACK:

1. WRISTWATCH
2. TRASH BAG
3. SUPER GLUE
4. CAYENNE PEPPER
5. SALT PACKET
6. ID CARD
7. TIN CAN
8. SOCKS
9. DUCT TAPE
10. NEWSPAPER

Hacks from Your Pack

SALT PACKET

Salt will relieve the pain of bug bites. Apply salt directly to the area affected.

Hacks from Your Pack

ID CARD

Remove bee and wasp stingers. Drag the ID card along the affected skin and it will flick the stinger right out of your skin.

IN THE PACK:

1. WRISTWATCH
2. TRASH BAG
3. SUPER GLUE
4. CAYENNE PEPPER
5. SALT PACKET
6. ID CARD
7. TIN CAN
8. SOCKS
9. DUCT TAPE
10. NEWSPAPER

37

CHALLENGE 6:
LIGHT A FIRE

IT'S IMPORTANT TO LIGHT A FIRE AT NIGHT. THE FIRE NOT ONLY KEEPS YOU WARM, BUT IT WILL ALSO ALLOW YOU TO COOK AND BOIL WATER, WHICH IS IMPERATIVE FOR KILLING PARASITES AND BACTERIA.

MAKE A PRIMITIVE OVEN

 STEP 1 Heat six to eight medium-sized rocks directly in your fire for two to three hours.

 STEP 2 Dig a hole in the dirt one foot deep and two feet across.

 STEP 3 Carefully move the hot rocks into the hole using a tree branch.

 STEP 4 Wrap your fish several times over in large, green leaves and tie it off with vine. Banana tree leaves are large and safe to use.

 STEP 5 Set the wrapped fish on top of the rocks and cover it all with dirt.

 STEP 6 After about an hour, dig up the fish, and enjoy your cooked meal.

IN THE PACK:

1. WRISTWATCH
2. TRASH BAG
3. SUPER GLUE
4. CAYENNE PEPPER
5. SALT PACKET
6. ID CARD
7. TIN CAN
8. SOCKS
9. DUCT TAPE
10. NEWSPAPER

HOW TO MAKE A FIRE

STEP 1
Gather dry wood. In the jungle, low-hanging tree branches tend to be drier than branches lying on the ground. Gather a variety of sizes, from twigs to large branches.

STEP 2
Place balled-up newspaper near small twigs or dry palm leaves.

STEP 3
Start a fire using friction by rubbing two pieces of wood together quickly.

Hacks from Your Pack

NEWSPAPER

Newspaper can be used for fast-burning tinder once you are ready to light your fire.

REAL-LIFE SURVIVAL STORY

Jungle Plane Crash

In 1971, seventeen-year-old Juliane Koepcke was the lone survivor of a ninety-two-passenger flight that crashed in the Peruvian rainforest. She remembered her father's advice to always travel downhill in the jungle because that leads to water, which leads to civilization. After bushwhacking through the forest for ten days with only a bag of candy to eat, surviving a maggot infestation in her arm, and successfully escaping local predators such as crocodiles and piranhas, Juliane encountered a hut and waited for the inhabitant to return. The next day, a hunter discovered the weak and injured teenager, fed her, treated her wounds, and helped her reunite with her father.

"Luckily, I'd lived in the jungle long enough as a child to be acquainted with the bugs and other creatures that scurry, rustle, whistle, and snarl. There was almost nothing my parents hadn't taught me about the jungle. I only had to find this knowledge in my concussion-fogged head."

BUGGIN' OUT!

One of the biggest foes you'll face in the jungle is the armies of insects that will feel as though they are constantly at war with you. But there are a few precautions you can take to make sure you're one step ahead of the bugs.

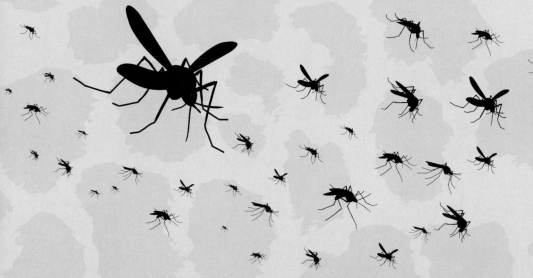

- Keep your clothes off the jungle floor or you could find spiders and ants lurking inside. Use a duct tape cord to tie between two trees to make a clothesline to hang up your clothes.

- Keep your footwear and clothes on when you get into the water.

PROTECT YOURSELF FROM MOSQUITOS

Did you know that malaria has caused more deaths than all the wars in history combined? If don't protect yourself from mosquito bites, you could catch malaria too. In the jungle, using mosquito nets and repellant is the best way to prevent bites. If you don't have any mosquito repellent, tie a t-shirt over your head so that it hangs down, covering your neck.

For another layer of protection, rub mud on your exposed skin. Once it dries, it will form a crusty barrier against mosquitoes.

DESERT FACTS!

The average daytime temperature is 100°F (38°C) while at night the average temperature drops to a much colder 25°F (-3.8°C)! This means you have to be extra clever about staying cool in the daytime and snuggly warm at night. You also have to battle sunburn, heatstroke, dehydration, hunger, sandstorms, and insects, just to name some.

Surviving blazing daytime temperatures and cold nights with little water and food can be done. All you need are your smarts, a little know-how, and a few common items to help sustain yourself until help arrives.

STRANDED IN THE SAND?

OH NO!

On a school field trip, your bus takes a wrong turn and gets stuck in the sand in the Mojave Desert. You decide to be the hero and walk through the sand to look for help. But soon you find yourself lost without your classmates to guide you back to the bus. Now you'll have to survive using only the stuff inside your backpack.

YOUR CHALLENGES

IN YOUR BACKPACK, YOU HAVE AN UNUSUAL ASSORTMENT OF ODDS AND ENDS LIKE LIP BALM, COMICS, AND TEA BAGS. IF THESE EVERYDAY ITEMS SEEM MORE USEFUL IN CIVILIZATION THAN WHEN YOU'RE LOST IN THE DESERT, THINK AGAIN. THEY ALL HAVE DOUBLE OR TRIPLE USES THAT CAN HELP YOU ENDURE ANYTHING MOTHER NATURE THROWS AT YOU.

Challenge **1**	**STAY HYDRATED**
Challenge **2**	**CREATE SHADE**
Challenge **3**	**START A FIRE**
Challenge **4**	**KEEP YOUR HUNGER IN CHECK**
Challenge **5**	**PROTECT YOUR SKIN**
Challenge **6**	**WEATHER A DUST STORM**

Hacks from Your Pack

IN THE PACK:

1. BANDANA
2. CHEWING GUM
3. GLASS BOTTLE
4. TEA BAGS
5. LIP BALM
6. SHOELACES
7. COMIC BOOKS
8. PONCHO

CHALLENGE 1:
STAY HYDRATED

IF YOUR WATER SUPPLIES ARE LOW, YOU WILL NEED TO LOOK FOR MORE. YOU CANNOT EXPECT TO SURVIVE MORE THAN A FEW DAYS IF YOU RUN OUT OF WATER. YOU MUST DRINK AT LEAST THREE LITERS OF WATER PER DAY TO SURVIVE IN THE DESERT!

IN THE PACK:

1. BANDANA
2. CHEWING GUM
3. **GLASS BOTTLE**
4. TEA BAGS
5. LIP BALM
6. **SHOELACES**
7. COMIC BOOKS
8. PONCHO

Hacks from Your Pack

GLASS BOTTLE

If you do come across water in the desert, use extreme caution before you start gulping it down. Collect the water in a glass bottle then purify it by boiling it over a fire. Glass won't break in the boiling temperatures.

SHOELACES

Believe it or not, shoelaces can act like a wick to get water that's dripping down from rocks. Look for a slope of hard, non-porous rock, where rainwater would run into the soil.

GETTING WATER FROM STONE

STEP 1
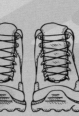
Take your shoelaces off your shoes.

STEP 2

Tie the ends together to make a loop.

STEP 3
Then twist the shoelaces together to make a cord.

STEP 4
Position it along a wet rock crevice.

STEP 5
As the rock gets waterlogged, the liquid will run down the shoelaces and drip at the end into your container (a water bottle or soda can works best).

STEP 6
Wait. It takes thirty minutes or longer to get enough water to drink.

FIVE ADDITIONAL WAYS TO FIND WATER

1. Collect dew gathering on plants before dawn.

2. Peek into hollow tree trunks for collected rainwater.

3. Follow animal tracks leading downhill, birds circling, or even flying insects.

4. Follow canyons or dry river beds upstream.

5. Dig about one foot (30 cm) down. If you feel any moisture, enlarge the hole and wait a few hours for the hole to fill with water.

CHALLENGE 2:
CREATE SHADE

IN A DESERT SURVIVAL SITUATION, YOU SHOULDN'T BE MOVING AROUND DURING THE DAY. SEEKING OUT SHADE OR MAKING A SHADE SHELTER CAN END UP SAVING YOU ¾ OF THE WATER REQUIRED PER DAY. ADDITIONALLY, BY KEEPING OUT OF THE SUN DURING THE DAY AND TRAVELING AT NIGHT DURING THE COOLER HOURS, YOU'LL BE ABLE TO TRAVEL FARTHER AND FASTER WITH MINIMUM DANGER OF HEAT EXHAUSTION.

IN THE PACK:

1. BANDANA
2. CHEWING GUM
3. GLASS BOTTLE
4. TEA BAGS
5. LIP BALM
6. SHOELACES
7. COMIC BOOKS
8. PONCHO

Hacks from Your Pack

BANDANA

Don't have a hat with you? Use a bandana to wrap your head instead. A bandana will cool you off when it's hot. This handy bit of cloth can also be used to strain water and as a tourniquet for bandaging a wound.

STEP 1

Using a stick, dig a trench in the sand that's three feet deep and long enough that you can fit your whole body inside.

STEP 2

Keep the sand you've dug out to make a tall boundary surrounding the hole.

STEP 3

Cover the top of the hole with the poncho.

STEP 4

Add sand around the edges of the poncho to keep it secure and from caving in.

IN THE PACK:

1. BANDANA
2. CHEWING GUM
3. GLASS BOTTLE
4. TEA BAGS
5. LIP BALM
6. SHOELACES
7. COMIC BOOKS
8. PONCHO

Hacks from Your Pack

PONCHO

Use a poncho to make a shade shelter. This shelter will keep the temperature 20 to 40°F cooler than the outside temperature!

THE DANGERS OF HEAT EXHAUSTION

If you feel lightheaded or nauseous or your skin feels cool and clammy, you'll need to find shade ASAP. Rest and loosen your clothing. Sipping on slightly salty water can also relieve symptoms.

If heat exhaustion isn't treated it can lead to heatstroke, which causes muscle cramping, red skin that no longer sweats, and, eventually, organ damage and death.

CHALLENGE 3:
START A FIRE

CONTRARY TO POPULAR BELIEF, DESERTS CAN GET BITTERLY COLD AT NIGHT. COLD TEMPERATURES CAN BE EXTREMELY DANGEROUS—ESPECIALLY IF YOU'RE ONLY WEARING SHORTS AND A T-SHIRT. THE WARMTH OF A FIRE CAN SAVE YOUR LIFE!

THREE REASONS TO START A FIRE

PREVENT HYPOTHERMIA

Build a fire at night when temperatures drop drastically.

PROTECT YOURSELF FROM PREDATORS

Fires scare off nocturnal desert predators like coyotes, bobcats, and mountain lions.

GET RESCUED

Rescue crews can spot even the smallest of fires from long distances at night.

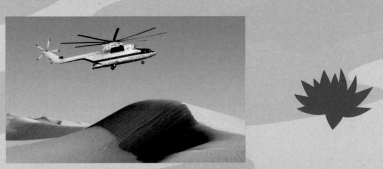

IN THE PACK:

1. BANDANA
2. CHEWING GUM
3. GLASS BOTTLE
4. TEA BAGS
5. LIP BALM
6. SHOELACES
7. COMIC BOOKS
8. PONCHO

Hacks from Your Pack

Use these three items to get a fire going quickly.

TEA BAGS

Dry out tea bags and use them for tinder under any sticks or large dead plants you can find to build a fire.

COMIC BOOKS

Superheroes don't just entertain—they can save your life when their stories are used to help start a fire. The paper from the books also makes great toilet paper.

LIP BALM

These waxy little sticks make a great emergency fuel source. Rub it onto cloth or even dried-out bark to make tinder that catches fire easily.

CHALLENGE 4: KEEP YOUR HUNGER IN CHECK

DON'T LISTEN TO YOUR GROWLING STOMACH. THE MORE YOU EAT, THE THIRSTIER YOU'LL GET, AND YOU COULD END UP DRINKING MORE WATER THAN YOU SHOULD.

IN THE PACK:

1. BANDANA
2. CHEWING GUM
3. GLASS BOTTLE
4. TEA BAGS
5. LIP BALM
6. SHOELACES
7. COMIC BOOKS
8. PONCHO

Hacks from Your Pack

CHEWING GUM

Use chewing gum as an appetite suppressant, or just a way to trick your mind into thinking it's getting food.

Chewing Gum

DO NOT EAT THESE!

Stay away from any plant with a milky sap. They are poisonous!

WHAT DO YOU EAT?

ONCE YOU FIND A WATER SOURCE, IT WILL BE SAFE TO EAT AGAIN. TRY THESE EDIBLE DESERT PLANTS!

The prickly pear cactus is about 85% water and has a high sugar and fiber content.

Desert Christmas cactus produces red berries with spines that can easily be scraped off. These berries taste a bit like strawberries and are a good source of vitamins C and A.

The very intimidating cholla cactus has flowers and seeds that can be eaten—just be extra careful of the spikes when picking off the edible parts.

Chia sage plants have purple spiky balls with tiny flowers and textured leaves that can all be eaten raw.

Agave plants—which look a little like aloe plants—have leaves, flowers, stalks, and seeds that are all edible.

Pinyon pine trees produce edible seeds called pine nuts that are delicious and full of nutrition.

53

CHALLENGE 5:
PROTECT YOUR SKIN

THE SUN IS A CONSTANT IN THE DESERT, BUT THAT DOESN'T MEAN YOU HAVE TO BURN TO A CRISP. SEVERE BURNS CAN LEAD TO INFECTION OR SUN POISONING. THE BEST WAY TO AVOID A SUNBURN IS TO STAY OUT OF THE SUN DURING THE DAY BY FINDING SHADE OR SEEKING SHELTER.

IN THE PACK:

1. BANDANA
2. CHEWING GUM
3. GLASS BOTTLE
4. TEA BAGS
5. **LIP BALM**
6. SHOELACES
7. COMIC BOOKS
8. PONCHO

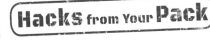

Hacks from Your Pack

LIP BALM

No SPF? Make your own homemade sunblock that will do in a pinch.

MAKESHIFT SUNSCREEN

While not as effective as regular sunscreen, using lip balm on your skin and lips will help protect your skin, as long as you're not in the sun all day. But don't get any in your eyes.

PREVENT BLISTERS

If there's a spot on your skin that is getting rubbed raw, put some lip balm on it to stop a painful blister from forming.

STOP BLEEDING

Apply lip balm to small cuts to stop bleeding. It will also keep out dirt and sand, which reduces the likelihood of infection.

CHALLENGE 6:
WEATHER A DUST STORM

DUST STORMS OCCUR WHEN STRONG WINDS COME ON SUDDENLY AND PICK UP DUST FROM THE GROUND AND OTHER SURFACES. THESE STORMS CAN BE UP TO ONE MILE HIGH AND TRAVEL OVER A HUNDRED MILES.

FOLLOW THESE STEPS:

Take cover near large rocks and boulders as soon as you see a storm approach.

Get to high ground. Dust storms tend to be less forceful at the top of a hill.

Protect your face with your arm as you move.

Sand ricochets around when it hits objects, therefore try to cover as much of your skin with clothing, a poncho, or even plants to minimize the area sand can come in contact with.

IN THE PACK:

1. BANDANA
2. CHEWING GUM
3. GLASS BOTTLE
4. TEA BAGS
5. LIP BALM
6. SHOELACES
7. COMIC BOOKS
8. PONCHO

Hacks from Your Pack

BANDANA

Fit a bandana over your mouth to keep you from breathing in dust during a storm. Covering your mouth with a bandana will also help to slow water loss from breathing, which helps you stay hydrated.

If a dust storm is severe enough, you could breathe in enough dust or sand to suffocate.

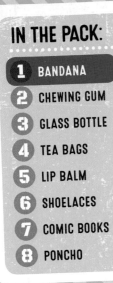

REAL-LIFE SURVIVAL STORY
Blindsided in the Desert

Mauro Properi was attempting to run an extreme desert marathon: a 6-day, 155-mile (250 km) marathon through the Sahara desert. Things went wrong on the fourth day of the marathon, when Mauro encountered a violent sandstorm. This sandstorm lasted eight hours, during which time Mauro was desperately trying to protect his face from the needle-like whipping of the sand for long enough to breathe.

When the storm abated, Mauro continued on what he thought was the marathon course . . . but it was the wrong direction. He only had a half a bottle of water with him. Survival in the extreme heat without enough to drink would be futile. In the ensuing days, he captured bats to drink their blood and even urinated into his empty bottle to use to rehydrate a bit. After ten days wandering off course, he encountered a young shepherd girl, who alerted the villagers about a strange man that needed help. Although Mauro had become severely ill and lost 35 lbs (16 kg) during his time lost in the desert, he made a full recovery and even returned four years later to finish the marathon.

LIFE IN THE
DESERT

While deserts feel like they are deserted, plenty of wildlife and plants thrive in their arid, hot conditions.

One of the most resilient animals living in the desert is the tortoise. An adult tortoise can tolerate temperatures in excess of 122°F (50°C) and can survive without water for up to one year.

A more treacherous desert resident is one of the most venomous scorpion species in the world—the deathstalker. This yellowish, translucent scorpion is found in the deserts of North Africa, the Middle East, and even some parts of North America. The deathstalker hunts mostly at night. Its sting is extremely painful with a venom toxic enough to kill a child or elderly person.

FOREST FACTS!

THERE ARE MORE THAN 60,000 TREE SPECIES ON THE PLANET. ALMOST EVERY TYPE OF TREE LIVES IN ONE OF THESE THREE TYPES OF FORESTS.

TROPICAL FORESTS

Warm, wet, and found near the equator.

TEMPERATE FORESTS

Cool, dry, and found mostly in the eastern United States, Canada, Europe, China, and Japan.

Forests are found on every continent on the planet!

BOREAL FORESTS (AKA SNOW FOREST)

A cold-climate forest found in Canada, Alaska, Sweden, Finland, Norway, and Russia.

LOST IN THE FOREST

OH NO!

You decided to spend a fun weekend with your family by taking a long hike in the forest. But as you stop to study an interesting-looking bug, you got separated and now you can't find anyone. Now you turn and turn and nothing looks familiar. The sun is starting to set and you begin to worry that you will not catch up with your family before it gets too dark. You'll have to use your wits to survive until help arrives.

YOUR CHALLENGES

IN YOUR BACKPACK, YOU HAVE AN EMPTY SODA CAN, A BALLOON, A MIRROR, DENTAL FLOSS, SHOELACES, TIGHTS, NEWSPAPER, AND BAKING SODA. IS ONE OF THESE ITEMS SECRETLY THE KEY TO SURVIVAL IN THE WILDERNESS?

Challenge 1   **GET DRINKABLE WATER**

Challenge 2   **START A FIRE**

Challenge 3   **NOTIFY OTHERS OF YOUR LOCATION**

Challenge 4   **STAY TICK-FREE**

Challenge 5   **BUILD A SHELTER**

Challenge 6   **FIND SOMETHING TO EAT**

Hacks from Your Pack

IN THE PACK:

1. BALLOON
2. WHISTLE
3. MIRROR
4. DENTAL FLOSS
5. TIGHTS
6. SODA CAN
7. SHOELACES
8. BAKING SODA
9. NEWSPAPER

CHALLENGE 1:
GET DRINKABLE WATER

COLLECTING WATER AND TRANSPORTING IT IS YOUR GOAL HERE—JUST DON'T FORGET THE CRUCIAL STEP OF PURIFYING IT BEFORE DRINKING, OTHERWISE YOU COULD DEHYDRATE FASTER DUE TO ILLNESS.

IN THE PACK:

1. BALLOON
2. WHISTLE
3. MIRROR
4. DENTAL FLOSS
5. TIGHTS
6. SODA CAN
7. SHOELACES
8. BAKING SODA
9. NEWSPAPER

Hacks from Your Pack

SODA CAN

Look for nearby birds. They like to fly around fresh water.

STEP 1
Use the can to collect water from a nearby clear-running stream.

STEP 2
Water isn't always safe to drink just because it looks clear and clean—now you must build a fire to boil it.

STEP 3
Purify the water by boiling it directly in the can over fire for at least five minutes.

Going down? Water often flows downhill.

IN THE PACK:

1 BALLOON
2 WHISTLE
3 MIRROR
4 DENTAL FLOSS
5 TIGHTS
6 SODA CAN
7 SHOELACES
8 BAKING SODA
9 NEWSPAPER

Hacks from Your Pack

BALLOON

A balloon is the perfect way to hold and transport water temporarily. Use the natural current of a stream or river to push water into the balloon mouth. Be careful when handling or it could unexpectedly burst, just like a water balloon.

TIGHTS

They may not keep your legs very warm, but they will filter water in a pinch. Pour the water you've collected through the fabric of your tights. The fabric will keep dirt and debris out of the water as it passes through. You should still purify the water before drinking it to remove harmful bacteria.

TERRAIN 04: FOREST

CHALLENGE 2:
START A FIRE

A FIRE IS ESSENTIAL FOR KEEPING YOU WARM, COOKING FOOD, PURIFYING WATER, AND EVEN SIGNALING YOUR LOCATION TO A RESCUE TEAM—SO YOU BETTER GET IT RIGHT! YOU'LL WANT TO START THE FIRE BEFORE YOU THINK YOU NEED IT, MAINLY BECAUSE IT'S EASIER TO START ONE WHEN YOU'RE CALM AND IT IS STILL LIGHT OUT.

STEP 1
Clear a wide area of forest floor around you. Layer kindling in a teepee shape on top of your newspaper or other tinder. Use tree bark like the papery outer layer of trees for kindling. It burns well even in damp weather.

STEP 2
Light the tinder by angling your mirror and focusing the sun's rays onto your tinder.

STEP 3
Layer logs on top of the kindling. Find dead, mold-free, dry wood logs for the actual firewood. You will need a variety of wood logs in different sizes to maintain your fire.

STEP 4
Make sure that there is enough air flowing through the pieces of wood to give your fire enough oxygen to keep burning for a long time. Watch the fire carefully and add a log or two every couple of hours.

STEP 5
Once your fire is started, you can place damp pieces of wood near the heat to dry out for future use.

Never leave a fire unattended!

Use your fire as a SOS signal during the day. Throw fresh grass or leaves on the fire to make it extra smoky.

IN THE PACK:

1. BALLOON
2. WHISTLE
3. MIRROR
4. DENTAL FLOSS
5. TIGHTS
6. SODA CAN
7. SHOELACES
8. BAKING SODA
9. NEWSPAPER

Hacks from Your Pack

MIRROR

Point at the sun to reflect the rays onto tinder to ignite it.

Hacks from Your Pack

NEWSPAPER

Easy-to-burn newspaper will come in handy as tinder to start your fire. Dead leaves, grass, pine needles, and shredded tree bark also make excellent tinder.

BAKING SODA

This is a handy tool for putting out fires before you go to sleep for the evening. If your fire has gotten out of hand, just throw it on the flames and they will quickly dwindle. Forest fires can spread quickly.

IN THE PACK:

1. BALLOON
2. WHISTLE
3. MIRROR
4. DENTAL FLOSS
5. TIGHTS
6. SODA CAN
7. SHOELACES
8. BAKING SODA
9. NEWSPAPER

CHALLENGE 3: NOTIFY OTHERS OF YOUR LOCATION

ALWAYS STAY PUT WHEN YOU'RE LOST. PEOPLE WILL BE MORE LIKELY TO FIND YOU IF YOU STAY IN ONE SPOT. THE MORE YOU ROAM FROM WHERE YOU STARTED, THE HARDER YOU WILL BE TO LOCATE. STAYING IN ONE PLACE ALSO REDUCES THE ENERGY YOUR BODY USES AND THE AMOUNT OF WATER AND FOOD YOU WILL NEED FOR ENERGY.

IN THE PACK:

1. BALLOON
2. WHISTLE
3. MIRROR
4. DENTAL FLOSS
5. TIGHTS
6. SODA CAN
7. SHOELACES
8. BAKING SODA
9. NEWSPAPER

Hacks from Your Pack

MIRROR

Even the smallest of mirrors can be used to reflect sunlight in multiple directions, which may get the attention of someone far away. Use the mirror multiple times during the sunniest part of the day for maximum effect.

IN THE PACK:

1. BALLOON
2. **WHISTLE**
3. MIRROR
4. DENTAL FLOSS
5. TIGHTS
6. SODA CAN
7. SHOELACES
8. BAKING SODA
9. NEWSPAPER

Hacks from Your Pack

WHISTLE

Blowing a whistle (or even loudly whistling using just your mouth) provides a sound signal to a rescue team so that they will find you faster.

- Even if you don't hear any signs of anyone nearby, keep calling out for help just in case someone hears it. Shout out for help as often as possible—preferably three times in a row at a time—so people can hear you even if they can't catch your voice the first time around.

- If you can't use a whistle, bang rocks together, shout or sing to signify that you are in the area.

CHALLENGE 4:
STAY TICK-FREE

WOODED AREAS LIKE FORESTS HAVE A VERY HIGH RISK OF TICK INFESTATION. A TICK IS A FLAT, LEATHERY, BLOODSUCKING ARACHNID THE SIZE OF A SESAME SEED THAT OFTEN DWELLS IN TREES OR ON LOW BUSHES, WAITING TO ATTACH ITSELF TO A PASSING ANIMAL OR PERSON. MANY TICKS CARRY DANGEROUS DISEASES SUCH AS LYME DISEASE.

Check your body frequently for burrowing ticks—especially your scalp and behind your ears. Ticks prefer warm, moist areas of the body, so double-check your armpits while you're at it.

IN THE PACK:

1. BALLOON
2. WHISTLE
3. MIRROR
4. DENTAL FLOSS
5. **TIGHTS**
6. SODA CAN
7. SHOELACES
8. BAKING SODA
9. NEWSPAPER

Hacks from Your Pack

TIGHTS

This tip is well-worn among military men and women: wear tights all the time, even under clothing, to help prevent ticks. Wearing tights makes it very hard for ticks to latch onto skin. Not only will wearing tights prevent bites, it also reduces blisters on your feet.

MORE ANTI-TICK TIPS

Wearing boots, long pants, long-sleeved shirts, and hats can also help prevent ticks from getting close to your skin. Try tucking your shirt into pants and the pant legs into your socks. You might not look hip, but you'll be bug-free.

CHALLENGE 5:
BUILD A SHELTER

YOU NEED TO MAKE A SHELTER THAT WILL REPEL WATER, BLOCK WIND, AND CREATE SHADE. BUT YOUR MASTERPIECE WILL QUICKLY BECOME A MESS IF IT DOESN'T STAY STANDING.

STEP 1

Build an A-frame shelter by stacking large branches against a standing tree.

STEP 2

Lash the large branches together using your shoelaces.

STEP 3

Stack brush, large leaves, and other plants over the large branches to make your walls.

STEP 4

Make some cozy bedding using piles and piles of soft leaves.

IN THE PACK:

1. BALLOON
2. WHISTLE
3. MIRROR
4. DENTAL FLOSS
5. TIGHTS
6. SODA CAN
7. **SHOELACES**
8. BAKING SODA
9. NEWSPAPER

Hacks from Your Pack

SHOELACES

They keep your shoes from slipping off your feet, but they can also be the perfect tool in helping to secure branches for a makeshift shelter.

KEEP AWAY FROM CAVES!

Don't be too quick to seek shelter for the night inside a cave. Predatory animal residents like bears and big cats might have the same idea. Unless you want a dangerous roomie, look for large rock outcroppings and fallen trees for shelter instead.

CHALLENGE 6:
FIND SOMETHING TO EAT

YOU CAN GO MORE THAN FOUR WEEKS WITHOUT EATING, BUT THAT DOESN'T MEAN YOU SHOULD.

HUNGRY?

Fishing isn't for everyone. If it proves too difficult, search for familiar nuts and berries to supplement your meal.

Blueberries and blackberries are safe to eat and plentiful. Avoid eating any berries that you are not familiar with—they could be poisonous.

Edible plants native to temperate forests are too numerous to name! Familiar plants like violet flowers, dandelion flowers, and clover are all tasty.

Nuts like hazelnuts, walnuts, and acorns only need a bit of elbow grease to coax the meat out of their shell. Try banging the nut against a boulder.

Don't be afraid to eat insects and other bugs. Avoid eating caterpillars, brightly-colored insects, or any insect that can bite or sting you. Be sure to cook the insects to kill any parasites, and remove the legs, head, and wings of any insect before eating.

Skip foraging for mushrooms. You will likely come across a variety of wild mushrooms in the forest, but it can be very difficult to tell the difference between edible and toxic wild mushrooms. It's better to be hungry than to eat something that will make you sick.

Crickets are a great food source—in fact, fifteen large crickets would be enough to meet your basic nutritional requirements for a day.

IN THE PACK:

1. BALLOON
2. WHISTLE
3. MIRROR
4. DENTAL FLOSS
5. TIGHTS
6. SODA CAN
7. SHOELACES
8. BAKING SODA
9. NEWSPAPER

Hacks from Your Pack

SODA CAN

Using the soda can tab from your soda can will make a fish hook good enough to grab that meal.

DENTAL FLOSS

Dental floss is sturdy and water-resistant, perfect to use for a makeshift fishing line.

STEP 1

Make your fish hook by cutting an opening of the bottom hole in the tab. Cut in at a slant, then cut away as much metal as possible around the hook.

STEP 2

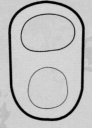

File the hook into a sharp point using a rock.

STEP 3

Tie a length of floss through the hole.

STEP 4

Tie the other end of the floss to a stick to serve as a fishing pole.

REAL-LIFE SURVIVAL STORY
Fun Hike Turns Chilling

While camping with his Boy Scout troop, a twelve-year-old wandered away from his campsite, got turned around, and became lost in the wilderness. Although he had no food or water, he drank from streams, curled up under rocks, and had enough clothing on to survive freezing overnight temperatures.

FOUND

The boy's disappearance kicked off an intensive search involving bloodhounds, heat-seeking helicopters, and dozens of volunteers on foot. After four days in the mountain wilderness, he was found weak and dehydrated, but physically fine. The boy's dad credits the book *Hatchet* by Gary Paulsen for helping his son survive. *Hatchet*, which is his son's favorite book, is the story of a boy whose plane crashes in the wilderness and how the boy learns to survive.

Search and rescue volunteers combing the North Carolina woods in search of a missing twelve-year-old boy.

TERRAIN 05: TROPICAL ISLAND

TROPICAL ISLAND FACTS!

 Tropical islands cover only two percent of the Earth's surface but are home to one-half of the world's animals and plants.

 There are currently many uninhabited tropical islands around the world. They remain deserted by humans due to a toxic climate, harsh living conditions, volcanic activity, or because they're considered protected space for endangered animals.

 Ōkunoshima Island, off the coast of Japan, is home solely to wild bunnies!

You could buy your own private tropical island! Lisbon Island, Portugal, goes for a cool $310 million.

TRAPPED IN THE TROPICS!

OH NO!

While you're on vacation sailing off the coast of Fiji, an unexpected storm hits. You are thrown from the boat into the Pacific Ocean—but don't worry, you swim your way to safety. You end up on an island you don't recognize.

Spending time relaxing on a palm tree-lined beach with the tropical blue ocean cooling your feet sounded like the perfect holiday . . . now you're stranded without a way to communicate with the outside world. What do you do when you are stuck all alone on an island, without food, water, and shelter?

YOUR CHALLENGES

REUSING COMMON ITEMS IN YOUR PACK FOR BASIC TASKS LIKE STARTING A FIRE, COLLECTING DRINKING WATER, AND BUILDING A SHELTER IS EASIER THAN YOU MAY THINK. DUCT TAPE, PAPER CLIPS, CRAYONS, OR EVEN A FRISBEE COULD HELP YOU SURVIVE WHILE STRANDED ON A REMOTE ISLAND. BUT WHICH ITEMS WILL YOU CHOOSE TO MAKE LIFE EASIER WHILE YOU WAIT FOR A RESCUE TEAM TO FIND YOU?

Challenge 1 > **GET DRINKABLE WATER**

Challenge 2 > **LIGHT YOUR WAY**

Challenge 3 > **GO FISHING**

Challenge 4 > **FIX INJURIES**

Challenge 5 > **BUILD A SHELTER**

Challenge 6 > **BUILD A COMPASS**

Hacks from Your Pack

IN THE PACK:

1. PONCHO
2. TIN CAN
3. METAL PAPER CLIPS
4. DENTAL FLOSS
5. DUCT TAPE
6. CRAYONS
7. FRISBEE
8. SILK HANDKERCHIEF

CHALLENGE 1: GET DRINKABLE WATER

YOU MIGHT BE SURROUNDED BY THE OCEAN, BUT YOU CAN'T DRINK SALT WATER. IF YOU DO, YOU COULD SUFFER EXTREME HEALTH RISKS INCLUDING CRIPPLING HEADACHES, VOMITING, THIRST, DEHYDRATION, BRAIN DAMAGE, AND ORGAN FAILURE.

DON'T DESPAIR, THOUGH. IF YOU ARE STRANDED ON A LARGE ISLAND, YOU'RE LIKELY TO FIND A FRESHWATER STREAM OR WATERFALL—THAT'S THE BEST PLACE TO GET WATER WORTH DRINKING. AND AS ALWAYS, MAKE SURE YOU BOIL STREAM WATER BEFORE DRINKING IT.

IN THE PACK:

1. PONCHO
2. TIN CAN
3. METAL PAPER CLIPS
4. DENTAL FLOSS
5. DUCT TAPE
6. CRAYONS
7. FRISBEE
8. SILK HANDKERCHIEF

Hacks from Your Pack

FRISBEE, TIN CAN & PONCHO

To build a solar still, you'll use the Frisbee as a makeshift shovel. Then you'll trap evaporating water with your poncho, which will run down the sides and collect in the tin can. After a few hours, you'll have drinkable water!

BUILD A MOISTURE TRAP

A moisture trap, or solar still, uses heat from the sun to evaporate and distill dirty water. This is handy if you don't want to wait for rainfall or can't find water inland. It's also one of the few instances where you can drink water collected without boiling it first.

STEP 1

Dig a hole in the ground three feet deep and four feet wide using your Frisbee as a shovel.

STEP 2

At the center of the hole, dig a deeper depression about the size of your tin can. Place the can in the hole.

STEP 3

Put fresh leaves and other plants in the hole surrounding your tin can. The plants will produce more moisture as the hole heats up.

STEP 4

Drape your plastic poncho over the entire hole and place rocks on the edges to keep in place.

STEP 5

Place another rock in the center of the poncho, just above the container.

STEP 6

Moisture will build up inside the pit from the heat and leaves. This will cause water to condense on the poncho and drip into the container.

STEP 7

After a few hours, collect the water from the tin can to drink.

CHALLENGE 2: LIGHT YOUR WAY

MAKING A FIRE NOT ONLY KEEPS YOU WARM AT NIGHT AND ENABLES YOU TO COOK, BUT IT ALSO SERVES AS A LIGHT BEACON FOR YOUR WOULD-BE RESCUE PARTY.

IN THE PACK:

1. PONCHO
2. TIN CAN
3. METAL PAPER CLIPS
4. DENTAL FLOSS
5. DUCT TAPE
6. CRAYONS
7. FRISBEE
8. SILK HANDKERCHIEF

Hacks from Your Pack

CRAYONS

Once you have a roaring fire, why not candles too? Make emergency candles using the crayons from your pack!

 STEP 1 Heat the bottom of a crayon over a flame so it will melt a little.

 STEP 2 Press the bottom of the crayon to a hard surface until the wax hardens so it will stay upright.

 STEP 3 Light the top.

 STEP 4 Once the flame gets going, the crayon will burn for fifteen to thirty minutes.

THE FIRE PLOW METHOD

Keep your fire as close to shore as possible so smoke can be seen by passing planes and boats.

Just because you don't have matches doesn't mean you can't have a roaring fire. Using some determination, you can light a fire using this friction method. All you need is a log of soft wood and a hard stick.

 STEP 1   Dig a groove into the soft wood log with the stick.

 STEP 2   Place quick-lighting tinder, such as paper or dried leaves, on the end of the soft wood that you want to ignite.

STEP 3   Move the stick up and down the groove very quickly to create friction.

STEP 4   When you see smoke forming around the tinder, blow on it to make the flames bigger.

 STEP 5   Place small, dry twigs on top of the flame to help encourage a larger fire.

85

CHALLENGE 3:
GO FISHING

BEING SO CLOSE TO WARM WATER MEANS YOU HAVE A WHOLE OCEAN OF MARINE LIFE TO EAT. THE FISH THAT LIVE IN THE SHALLOW POOLS AT THE BEACH ARE USUALLY THE EASIEST TO CATCH.

SIX TOXIC TROPICAL FISH TO AVOID

Whatever you do, don't eat these fish!

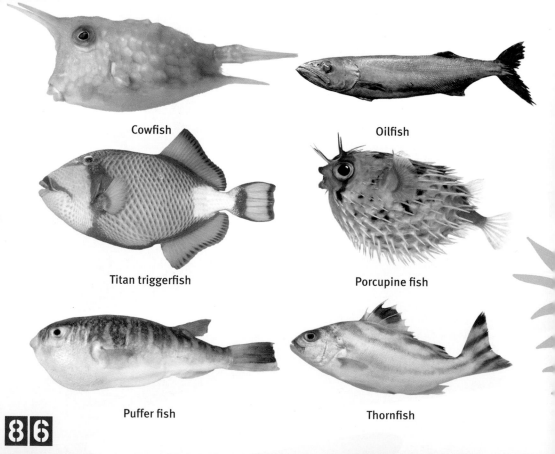

Cowfish

Oilfish

Titan triggerfish

Porcupine fish

Puffer fish

Thornfish

IN THE PACK:

1. PONCHO
2. TIN CAN
3. METAL PAPER CLIPS
4. DENTAL FLOSS
5. DUCT TAPE
6. CRAYONS
7. FRISBEE
8. SILK HANDKERCHIEF

DENTAL FLOSS & PAPER CLIPS

Dental health is important, but did you know dental floss can help you snag your next meal? Using a paper clip as a hook and floss as the line, you have everything you need to go fishing!

STEP 1

Bend the paper clip into a S-shape.

STEP 2

Measure a length of dental floss. Knot one side of the paper clip. Tie the floss through the knotted end of the clip.

STEP 3

Using a rock, sharpen the hook end of the paperclip.

STEP 4

Fasten a fly or worm at the end of the paperclip to use as bait.

BONUS HACK:
CRACK A COCONUT

On a tropical island one of the more abundant edible fruits you might spot is the coconut. The white, fleshy meat is nutritious and is rich in oil. To break the tough husk, find a large rock and drop it straight down onto the pointy end of the coconut. Then turn the coconut over and throw the rock at the blunt end, which should do the trick.

Next, find the ridge line on the inner coconut. Bang the inner coconut at the middle of that ridge line against a sharp rock to split it open. Pop it open to get to the coconut water and meat.

CHALLENGE 4: FIX INJURIES

CHANCES ARE AT SOME POINT YOU WILL INJURE YOURSELF FISHING, BUILDING SHELTER, OR JUST TRYING TO OPEN A COCONUT. BUT YOU HAVE ONE MIRACLE TOOL IN YOUR PACK THAT'S PERFECT FOR MANY FIRST AID NEEDS!

IN THE PACK:

1. PONCHO
2. TIN CAN
3. METAL PAPER CLIPS
4. DENTAL FLOSS
5. DUCT TAPE
6. CRAYONS
7. FRISBEE
8. SILK HANDKERCHIEF

Hacks from Your Pack

DUCT TAPE

BUTTERFLY BANDAGE

Rip off two small strips of duct tape and connect them to a smaller strip by touching the sticky side of the smaller strip to the sticky side of the larger strips. Then apply to the wound.

BANDAGE

For larger wounds, apply soft cloth ripped from your T-shirt or another piece of clothing. Wrap some duct tape around the injured body part to hold the cloth in place.

BROKEN BONES

A splint will stabilize a broken limb.

 STEP 1 Wrap padding like a T-shirt around the injured limb.

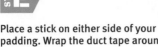 **STEP 2** Place a stick on either side of your padding. Wrap the duct tape around both the sticks to secure them. Be careful not to make it too tight.

SPRAINED ANKLE OR WRIST

Wrap your injured joint with a thin layer of padding from a piece of clothing. Pull duct tape securely around the padding. This will give your sprain some much-needed support.

SPLINTERS

Place duct tape on top of the splinter stuck in your skin. Press hard to ensure the tape is grabbing the splinter. Then rip off in the same direction the splinter is facing. The splinter should stick to the tape.

SIGNALING FOR HELP

If you are severely injured, signaling for help is one of the most important things you can do.

Write the letters SOS (the international code signal of extreme distress) on the sand close to the shore with the help of some large branches or large rocks. The letters must be large enough that they can be seen from the air.

SOS is an ambigram—a word that looks identical whether read upside-down or right-side-up. This is helpful for rescue helicopters and planes to see no matter what direction they are coming from.

CHALLENGE 5: BUILD SHELTER

EVEN IN A WARM, PLEASANT CLIMATE, YOU'LL STILL NEED TO BUILD A SHELTER TO PROTECT YOU FROM SUDDEN WEATHER CHANGES AND CURIOUS ANIMALS.

Hacks from Your Pack

DENTAL FLOSS

Use dental floss as the string that will bind your branches and make sturdy walls.

BUILD A TEEPEE

This cone-shaped type of shelter is easy to build and uses many materials already on the island.

STEP 1

Find ten to twenty long, thick branches, all around the same length.

STEP 2

Stick three of the branches into the ground in an imaginary circle, all angled toward each other.

STEP 4

Leaving room for a doorway, place the remaining branches in a circle around the tripod so they are all leaning against the first three branches.

STEP 3

Tie the tops together with dental floss.

STEP 4

Cover the stick structure with leaves and other plant life for protection.

CHALLENGE 6: BUILD A COMPASS

FIGURING OUT WHICH DIRECTION YOU'RE FACING WILL HELP YOU GET BACK TO HOME BASE AFTER TRAVELING AROUND THE ISLAND. IF YOU DON'T HAVE A MAGNET HANDY, YOU CAN MAGNETIZE A PAPERCLIP USING THIS EASY METHOD!

IN THE PACK:

1. PONCHO
2. TIN CAN
3. METAL PAPER CLIPS
4. DENTAL FLOSS
5. DUCT TAPE
6. CRAYONS
7. FRISBEE
8. SILK HANDKERCHIEF

Hacks from Your Pack

METAL PAPERCLIP & SILK HANKERCHIEF

STEP 1

Unfold the paperclip and sharpen one end into a point using a rock.

STEP 2

Magnetize your paper clip by quickly rubbing it in one direction (towards the pointy end) against a silk handkerchief.

STEP 3

Fill your tin can with water and place the leaf gently on top of the water so it's floating.

STEP 4

The magnetized paperclip should pull the floating leaf clockwise or counter-clockwise to orient itself. The pointy end will point toward north.

REAL-LIFE SURVIVAL STORY
A Family Adrift

A Scottish sailor, his wife, and four young children were sailing to the Galapagos Islands when a pod of killer whales sank their boat. The family scrambled on board an inflatable life raft, where they survived by catching rainwater and hunting turtles and fish. They would use turtle blood to hydrate when they ran out of rainwater to drink and used the fat to rub on their skin for protection against the harsh sun. A Japanese fishing boat rescued them after a grueling 38 days adrift.

ANYTIME, ANYWHERE SURVIVAL TIPS

PREDATOR POINTERS

Bears

Be cautious of caves. It's possible that they are already occupied by hibernating bears and you would not want to disturb them. Your best way to scare off a bear is by making loud sounds. Make a shrill yell sound that should frighten your unwanted visitor away.

Wolves

Wolves will only attack when they feel that they are being threatened. Keep your distance.

Snakes

Avoid reaching into small spaces or under rocks without poking it with a stick first. Scorpions, spiders, or snakes could be hiding there, and you don't want to startle them. If you do encounter one, give them space.

GET ORIENTED

Pick a home base. Find a way to mark it using a piece of clothing easily visible from a distance.

Determine where north, south, east, and west are. The sun rises in the east and sets in the west. If you want to walk south in the morning, the sun will be on your left (east).

Look for any landmarks that you might recognize and try to remember what direction they are in relation to you.

Listen for familiar sounds, such as running water or traffic noise, that might give you clues as to where you are.

RECOGNIZE FROSTBITE

Wear mittens rather than gloves and don't lace your footwear too tightly. If your skin turns white or you feel a stinging sensation from a breeze, you are likely suffering from frostbite.

C.O.L.D.? DRESS IN LAYERS!

This acronym will help you remember these four tips:

Clean (skin)
(Avoid) Overheating
(Wear) Loose layers
(Stay) Dry

Overheating is a major danger, as your inner layer of clothing will absorb your sweat, which will then make you colder. Open your coat and remove a thin inner layer of clothing if you start to get too hot. Loose layers of clothing help keep you warm and dry.

HOT? DRESS IN LAYERS!

If you're in a sunny terrain, wear sunglasses, a hat, and apply charcoal or campfire ashes around your eyes to deflect the sun's glare.

Skip the shorts and tank tops. Wearing loose clothes that cover your whole body helps you avoid sunburn and keep cool. Cover up your arms, legs and face as best you can.

A COMPASS IN THE WILD

HOW TO MAKE A COMPASS USING ONLY A NEEDLE AND MAGNET

WHAT YOU NEED:

Needle

Magnet

Large leaf

INSTRUCTIONS:

STEP 1 Drag the needle across the magnet from head to tip. Repeat twenty to thirty times to polarize it.

STEP 2 Place the polarized needle on a leaf.

STEP 3 Set the leaf on top of a still body of water like a puddle. The head of the needle will orient itself so it's pointing north.

TIP: If you don't have a needle, you can use a nail, a bobby pin, or a safety pin.

S — N

INDEX

B

Bag
    Sandwich 14
    Trash 31
    Tea 51
Baking soda 67
Balloon 65
Bandana 48, 57
Book 20

C

Can
    Soda 12, 14, 64, 75
    Tin 28, 83
Cayenne pepper 36
Chewing gum 52
Comic books 51
Crayon 85

D

Dental floss 75, 87, 91
Duct tape 35, 89

E

Eyeglasses 14

F

Frisbee 83

G

Glass bottle 46

H

Handkerchief, silk 92

I

ID card 37

L

Lip balm 51, 55

M

Mirror 67, 68

N

Newspaper 38, 67
Nickel 16

P

Paperclip, metal 87, 92
Poncho 49, 83

R

Ruler 18

S

Salt 37
Shoelaces 46, 73
Socks 29
Super glue 36

T

Tennis rackets 22
Tights 65, 71

W

Wristwatch 33
Whistle 69